Denied Doesn't Define

Verses To Help Overcome Denial And Rejection

Iris McClain

DENIED DOESN'T DEFINE

iUniverse books may be ordered through booksellers or by contacting:

iUniverse
1663 Liberty Drive
Bloomington, IN 47403
www.iuniverse.com
1-800-Authors (1-800-288-4677)

ISBN: 978-1-5320-8959-6 (sc)
ISBN: 978-1-5320-8972-5 (e)

Print information available on the last page.

iUniverse rev. date: 12/23/2019

Dedication

This book is dedicated to my mother, who always encouraged me to write and my sister who I used to tell my ideas about a new book or invention.

Acknowledgement

A thank you to my children, family and friends who have opened up their hearts and ears. A special thank you to those who have walked this journey with me.

Introduction to Injustice

Deniedactuponmotiongrantedjusticedueprocessattorney
fraudjurisdictionhear ingcontemptdebtorproseequitablefee
waivedreinstatedjudgejurybailiffgranted consentorderproof
ofclaimcircuitbankruptcycivilobjectiondiscovery7appealloa
nmodificationdocketedcourtmemoterminatedcaseadministrator
deficiencyame ndedcomplaintcountplannoticechapterclerkdebt
procedureunrepresentedobjec tioncreditoroppositionbias-
certificationdismissautomaticstaystatuteoflimitatio nsrule
lawopeningdenovoDENIEDDOESN'TDEFINEprimafacie
validityentere d341meetingofcreditorsorderedstrikeappearanc-
emovantappelleeconfirmation signedappellantreconsideration
llsecuredfiledextendmotiontranscriptdesignat ionrecordissues
onappealunsecureddisallowdeferredleavetrusteefileamendpap
ernodocketentrydefaultadversaryappendixsupremecourt
briefevidencesealedfa lsepetition13dischargevoidfinetranscript
interestratediscrepancydenyopencom plaintlawyerjusticefair-
resjudicataclosetestimonyerroneousharmlitigationaffir med
withoutprejudiceproceedingtimelyfiledfraudjurisdiction
securedbankrupc ytrusteeextendcertificateofservicetranscript
designationofrecordissuesperjury deferreddamagesstayabuse
ofdiscretionpunitivedistrictperjuryswornindefinedinjustice

By

Iris McClain

Verses To Help Overcome Denial And Rejection

Denied Doesn't Define

It means you tried

Again

They lied

Denied Doesn't Define

Your heart or your mind
The hidden face of injustice
Controlling the rulings that bind

Denied Doesn't Define

The unspoken agenda of the judges
They sit behind immunity
Their pen issues their grudges

Denied Doesn't Define

The door locked shut
Makes you more determined
Through it strut

Denied Doesn't Define

The job that pass us crept
We weren't as pretty or as light
What you see is what you get

Denied Doesn't Define

The twists and turns you take
When life puts you on a course
You never intended to undertake

Denied Doesn't Define

Whether you win or lose
The system is against you
Their abuse of power for you choose

Denied Doesn't Define

Their fraud they mask
Lack of training or education
We undertook the daunting task

Denied Doesn't Define

The hope inside
That helps us cope
When our loved one died

Denied Doesn't Define

It empowers us to be
What prejudice and injustice
Won't allow them to see

Denied Doesn't Define

Why your parents split
Not your fault
They no longer fit

Denied Doesn't Define

Our David v Goliath attitude
Approval is within
Rejection is their platitude

Denied Doesn't Define

The system is broken irreparably
An easy out for the creditor
The mask of prima facie validity

Denied Doesn't Define

The disadvantaged pro se litigant
Who lacks manpower and money
Limiting their effectiveness against the giant

Denied Doesn't Define

Inner beauty
That no break-up can destroy
It's good to be free

Denied Doesn't Define

Their arbitrary rulings-obviously wrong
Designed to defeat our self-esteem
Never! Because He makes us strong

Denied Doesn't Define

Being unfairly terminated
Because the boss feels
You're too complicated.

Denied Doesn't Define

The raise or bonus you didn't get
Because the CEO/COO
Wanted a new jet

Denied Doesn't Define

Working with no pay
The shutdown
Lasted another day

Denied Doesn't Define

Denied, a negative word
Meant to suppress and humiliate
Is too often heard

Denied Doesn't Define

The truth of the evidence they suppress
The ordeal itself
Is one of unrelenting stress

Denied Doesn't Define

Through their fraud, you they bleed
While they pay millions to the regulators
Who expose their greed

Denied Doesn't Define

Your fight to keep your house and car
The crooked Judges & Lawyers
They won't disbar

Denied Doesn't Define

It means you tried
And again
They lied

Denied Doesn't Define

your true value
don't feel you need to be validated
YOU validate YOU

Printed in the United States
By Bookmasters